FILM POSTERS of the 30s

the essential movies of the decade

from the reel poster gallery collection

edited by tony nourmand and graham marsh

EVERGREEN

EVERGREEN is an imprint of
TASCHEN GmbH

© 2005 TASCHEN GmbH
Hohenzollernring 53, D-50672 Köln

www.taschen.com

Produced by Aurum Press Ltd., London

© 2003 by Reel Poster Co. Ltd.

Art direction and design by Graham Marsh
Page make-up by Trevor Gray
Editorial Assistance by Kim Goddard
Text edited by Roxanna Hajiani

ISBN 978-3-8228-4511-0

Printed in Thailand

ACKNOWLEDGEMENTS

Alison Aitchison
Richard & Barbara Allen
Martin Bridgewater Collection
Joe Burtis
Glynn Callingham
Andrew Cohen Collection
Collection Atmosphere
Tony Crawley
The Crew From The Island
Chris Dark Collection
Greg Ferland
Leslie Gardner
Tamlyn Guy
Philip Halewood Collection
Sarah Hodgson
Intellectual Property Management Associates
Eric & Prim Jean-Baptise
Mike Kaplan
John & Billie Kisch
Jose Ma. Carpio
June Marsh
Hamid Joseph Nourmand
Gabriella Pantucci
Mark H. Wolff
X-Man

**And special thanks to
Bruce Marchant**

Horse Feathers (1932)
US 41 × 27 in. (104 × 69 cm)
(Re-release 1936)
Art by Constantin Alajálov

contents

what price hollywood?

Looking at the bright, colourful images in this book it is hard to remember, not only that the vast majority of 30s films were shot in black and white, but also that this was the decade of the Great Depression. For despite the hard economic times, or perhaps because of them, Hollywood's output was relentlessly upbeat, the focus was on escapism and entertainment. In 1933 there may have been soup kitchens on the streets of New York, but cinema goers' eyes were directed upwards to King Kong perched atop the Empire State Building; in 1939 it was not the story of the Okies' grim trek to California that caught the public's imagination but Dorothy's journey along the Yellow Brick Road in search of The Wizard of Oz; and that same year, as Europe threatened to burst into the flames of war, American audiences were more interested in watching Atlanta burn in Gone with the Wind.

But if the Hollywood studios could chose to ignore the grim realities of a world sunk in economic and political gloom, they could not disregard the activities of the Hayes Office, Hollywood's response to the growing demand for censorship, which culminated in 1934 with the introduction of the Hayes Code. The Code, which was much preoccupied with the minutiae of sex and other 'undesirable' activities, was modified and renamed over the years but continues to determine what can and cannot appear on American screens to this day. The studios, however, often saw the Code less as a constraint than as a challenge to their ingenuity; and in their effort to test the boundaries of acceptability to the limit, the poster artists of the 30s created work which are some of the most interesting ever produced. Look, for example, at the poster for The Bitter Tea of General Yen, released in 1933 just before the introduction of the Code. Although the film's leading lady, Barbara Stanwyck, featured in many major films that challenged the prevailing morality, neither Columbia Studios, nor probably Stanwyck herself, wanted her to be recognisable on the rather risque poster, which drove home its message with the tagline: 'They found a love they dared not touch'. In contrast, that same year, another studio, Warner Brothers, commissioned Alberto Vargas (pp. 17 & 91) to paint Stanwyck in her role as a gangster's moll for the poster promoting Ladies They Talk About; the resulting image left audiences in no doubt why the 'Ladies' in question were being discussed – no tagline required.

The maverick producer Howard Hughes began his struggles with the Hayes Office in 1930 over Hell's Angels. Battle was rejoined in 1932 when, after much deliberation, he allowed the censor's scissors to excise the more explicit activities of the gigolo pilot in Cock of the Air. In exchange, the Hayes Office agreed not to press their case against Scarface (1932). True, they did insist that the poster should carry the tagline 'The Shame of a Nation' but this did little to defuse the effect of an image showing the film's gangster hero, Paul Muni, using a sheriff's badge to light his cigarette. At the other end of the scale, Dwain Esper, a shrewd businessman and independent producer/director making films outside the studio system, was able to get away with drug films such as Marijuana (1934) by insisting that their purpose was to educate rather than titillate the public! Although cheaply and crudely made, his films, and their posters, have a period charm, almost innocence, of their own.

In Europe they did things more stylishly. Illustrator Roger Vacher's poster for Extase (1932) (p. 86), depicting Hedy Lamarr as a young woman in the throes of sexual awakening, made no pretence at educational value, though, interestingly, it did not feature Ms Lamarr's name. The most famous and admired French artist of the 30s, Jean Adrien Mercier (pp. 104 & 105) was responsible for the design for Rene Clair's 14 Juillet (1933), which is generally considered the best of the one hundred or so posters he created and would be included in many people's list of the best posters ever.

In Hollywood, studios were prepared to take talent wherever they could find it. For example, the American illustrator James Montgomery Flagg (pp. 44 & 45) who created the legendary campaign for Lost Horizon (1933), is probably best-known for his recruiting poster, used in both World Wars, showing the artist himself in the role of Uncle Sam, pointing a stern finger at the viewer with the blunt message 'I Want You'. But the field was becoming increasingly professionalized. The Warner Brothers poster graphics of the period, considered some of the best of all time, were mainly created under the supervision of art directors Anthony Gablik (pp. 56, 57, 62, 63, 82 & 119), Hubbard G. Robinson (pp. 24 & 25) and Joseph Tisman (pp. 24, 25, 56, 57, 62, 63, 82 & 119). Among the American one-sheets that stand out for the quality of their design are those for Public Enemy (1931), I Am a Fugitive from a Chain Gang (1932), 42nd Street (1933), Footlight Parade (1933), The Kennel Murder Case (1933), Private Detective 62 (1933), Bordertown (1935) and G-Men (1935). For a short period in the mid-30s the studios' own posters were supplemented by those created by Leader Press, an American company that offered cinema owners alternative designs, usually three-colour silk-screens. Among their classic creations were those featuring Jean Harlow in Riffraff (1936) and Ronald Colman as Clive of India (1935).

Comedy was, of course, one of the most popular genres of the time and two American poster artists, Al Hirschfeld (pp. 96, 97, 98, 99, 100 & 101) and Hap Hadley (pp. 46, 47 & 103) specialized in the field. Hirschfeld produced artwork for the Marx Brothers' films A Night at the Opera (1935) and A Day at the Races (1937), some early Three

What Price Hollywood? (1932)
US 41 x 27 in. (104 x 69 cm)

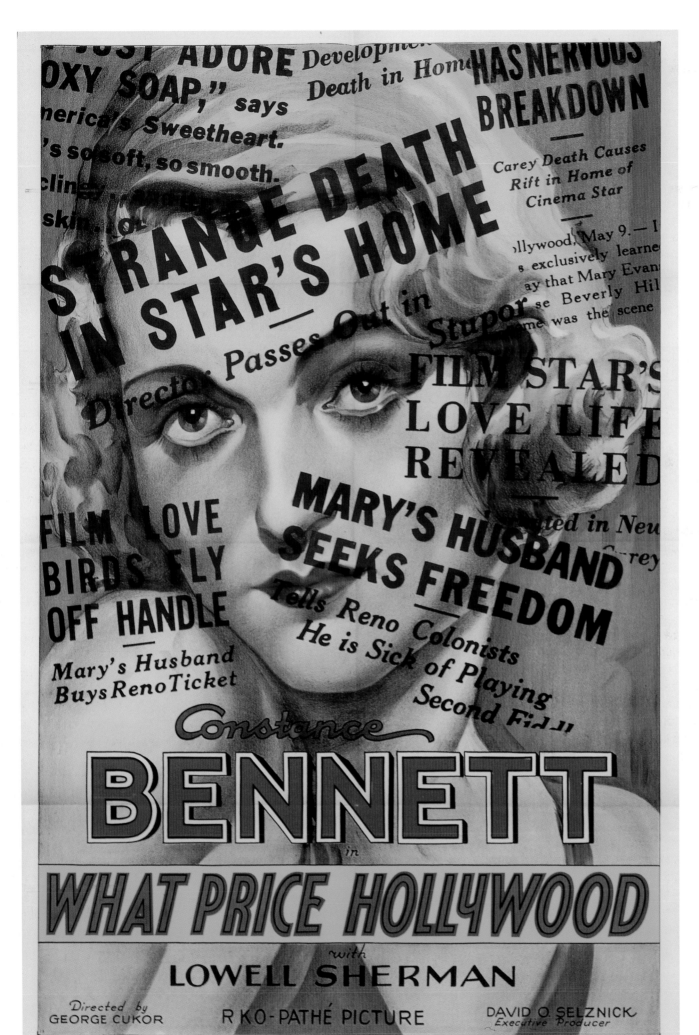

Stooges releases such as *Hello Pop* (1933), as well as a succession of Laurel and Hardy titles like *Another Fine Mess* (1930), *Beau Hunks* (1931) and *Pack Up Your Troubles* (1932). Hadley, who had designed posters for Chaplin films in the 20s, continued the good work with *City Lights* (1931) and widened his repertoire with posters for two Howard Hughes movies, *Hell's Angels* and *Cock of the Air*.

Another popular 30s genre, now long-forgotten, was the serial which, like its literary counterpart, aimed to lure audiences back by ending each installment with a cliff-hanger. The classic example of the successful serial was *Flash Gordon* (1936) and its appealing combination of Boys Own adventure and sci-fi was admirably captured in the poster, which launched the first installment of the sequence in the US. Nor should we overlook another vanished genre, the B movie of which literally thousands were produced in the course of the decade. By the time he rose to stardom with *Stagecoach* (1939), John Wayne had already played leading roles in over seventy B films, mostly Westerns. Posters for at least two of these, *Paradise Canyon* (1935) and *Oregon Trail* (1936), have subsequently become highly sought after by collectors. Interestingly, though, Wayne's image does not feature on the poster for *Stagecoach*.

Horror was something of a speciality for Universal, still a poverty-row studio at the beginning of the decade, and the resident artist, Karoly Grosz (pp. 8, 38 & 39) was responsible for the artwork for *Frankenstein* (1931) and *The Mummy* (1932). These Universal Horror releases did much to foster the studio's fortunes and the posters, few of which have survived, have become among the most sought after by present-day collectors. In 1993 an example of Grosz's *Frankenstein* poster set a new world record when it was sold at auction for $198,000, a figure which was comfortably exceeded four years later in 1997 when the same artist's poster for *The Mummy* was auctioned for $435,000, setting a record that still stands and, incidentally, is three times more than has ever been paid for the most desirable of Toulouse Lautrec's lithographs.

Other 30s posters which are rare and eagerly sought after include those for Hitchcock movies, particularly those designed for the British market. Like much other 'waste' paper, they were recycled during the war years and the British three-sheet for *The 39 Steps* (1935) is among the few survivors.

An important feature of 30s cinema, and one that contrasts strongly with the situation today, was the rich variety of meaty roles it offered to female stars; indeed, their pulling power was so crucial that they were often given pride of place in the poster campaigns. For example, the studio obviously reckoned that Constance Bennett was their key weapon in the campaigns for *Moulin Rouge* (1934), *Our Betters* (1937) and *What Price Hollywood?* (1932), which was re-made as *A Star is Born* in 1937, 1954 and 1976. Other instances of leading ladies deployed in close up are the posters featuring Carole Lombard in *Love Before Breakfast* (1936), Claudette Colbert in *She Married Her Boss* (1935), Bette Davis in *Bordertown* (1935) and *Jezebel* (1938), Greta Garbo in *Mata Hari* (1931) and *As You Desire Me* (1932), Gene Harlow in *The Red-Headed Woman* (1932) and Marlene Dietrich in *Shanghai Express* (1932), *The Devil is a Woman* (1935) and *Blonde Venus* (1932), in which she was portrayed as the Venus de Milo for the poster campaign.

When it came to Astaire and Rogers, who first teamed up in the musical extravaganza *Flying Down to Rio* (1933) and became inseparable with *Top Hat* (1935), there was, of course, no question but that both had to feature on the posters, only in combination could they suggest that mixture of glamour and escapism that audiences found so irresistible.

Black faces did not feature much on 30s posters, and indeed very little in 30s films except in minor roles as servants. The one exception was Paul Robeson, who first emerged in Black-cast films and went on to become the first Black superstar. His most famous 30s role was probably that of Brutus in *Emperor Jones* made in 1933, by which time his status with Black audiences had become iconic. The poster features his image no less than five times, showing the stages in his rise from slave to emperor. Later, for *Sanders of the River* (1935) the Argentinian artist Osvaldo Venturi (pp. 64 & 72) created a heroic portrait of Robeson as the very personification of the Noble Savage. Another African-American who succeeded in making his mark in the 30s cinema was Oscar Micheaux. He had already achieved the well-nigh incredible by becoming the first Black to produce a feature film, *The Homesteader* (1919), and his 1937 film *Underworld* was the first to treat the gangster theme from a Black perspective. By the time he produced the musical *Swing* in 1938 his following was immense, and he must share with Robeson the honour of having achieved what many would have thought impossible in an America that was still largely racially segregated,

Sixty years on, one can only be astonished that so unpromising a decade as the 30s should have bequeathed us such a rich legacy of cinematic treasures. And the posters, no less than the films themselves, still retain a surprising contemporary appeal. As this collection shows, the best of them remain surprisingly 'modern' and, perhaps, a good deal more stylish than their counterparts of today. Good poster art, it seems, like good film-making, is timeless.

TONY NOURMAND AND GRAHAM MARSH

Bringing Up Baby
(L'Impossible Monsieur Bébé) (1938)
French 63 × 47 in. (160 × 119 cm)
Art by Bernard Lancy

R K O RADIO FILMS S.A. Présente

KATHARINE HEPBURN - CARY GRANT

b.lancy

R K O RADIO FILMS

L'IMPOSSIBLE MONSIEUR BÉBÉ

Mise en scène de HOWARD HAWKS

R.K.O. RADIO FILMS S.A. 52, Champs Elysées - Paris - Bal, 54-55 et la suite - 1939

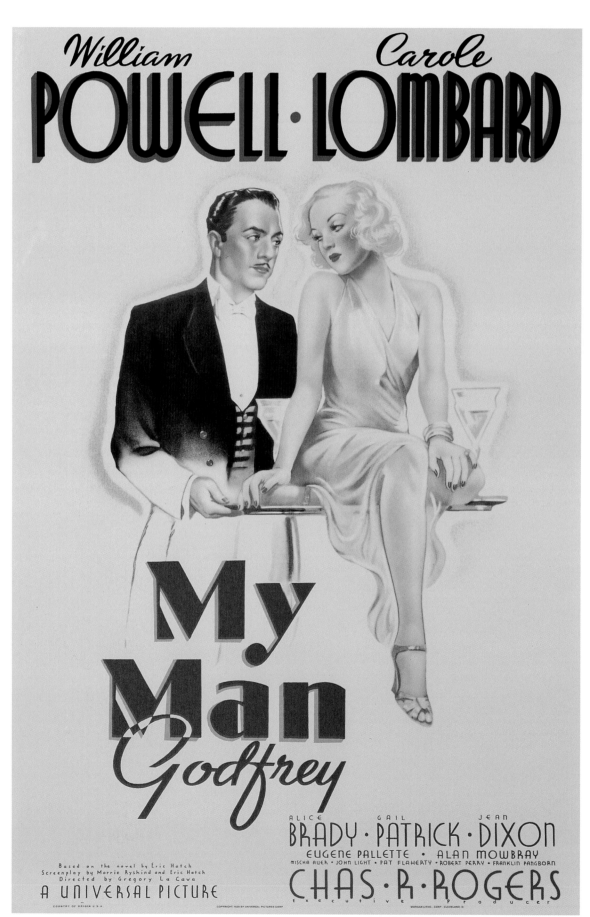

My Man Godfrey (1936)
US 41 × 27 in. (104 × 69 cm)
(Style C)
Art by Karoly Grosz

CARL LAEMMLE presents

Carole Lombard

Faith Baldwin's

LOVE BEFORE BREAKFAST

With **PRESTON FOSTER**

CESAR ROMERO · JANET BEECHER

FROM THE NOVEL "SPINSTER DINNER"

DIRECTED BY WALTER LANG · AN EDMUND GRAINGER PROD.

●

A universal picture

It Happened One Night (1934)
US 41 × 27 in. (104 × 69 cm)
(Style A)
Art direction by Jack Meyers

It Happened One Night (1934)
US 41 × 27 in. (104 × 69 cm)
(Style B)
Art direction by Jack Meyers

TOGETHER FOR
THE FIRST TIME!

CLARK   CLAUDETTE
GABLE *and* COLBERT
in
"*It Happened One Night*"
with WALTER CONNOLLY • ROSCOE KARNS
From the Cosmopolitan Magazine story by SAMUEL HOPKINS ADAMS • Screen play by ROBERT RISKIN

 a FRANK CAPRA PRODUCTION   A COLUMBIA PICTURE

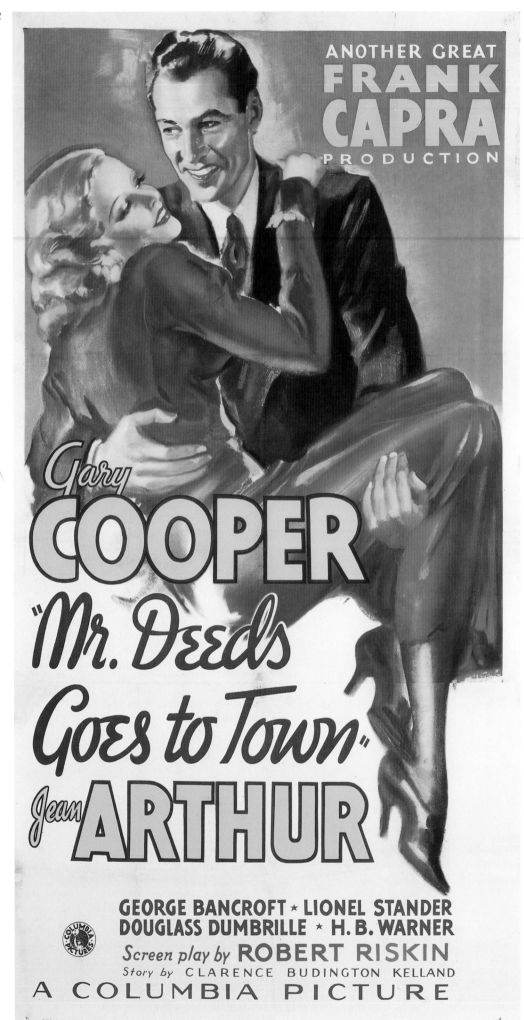

**Mr. Smith Goes To Washington
(Mr. Smith Va A Washington)** (1939)
Italian 79 × 55 in. (201 × 140 cm)
Art by Anselmo Ballester

Mr. Deeds Goes to Town (1936)
US 81 × 41 in. (206 × 104 cm)
Art direction by Jack Meyers

Un grande film di
FRANK CAPRA
(COLUMBIA)
con Jean
ARTHUR
James
STEWART

Mr. Smith va a Washington

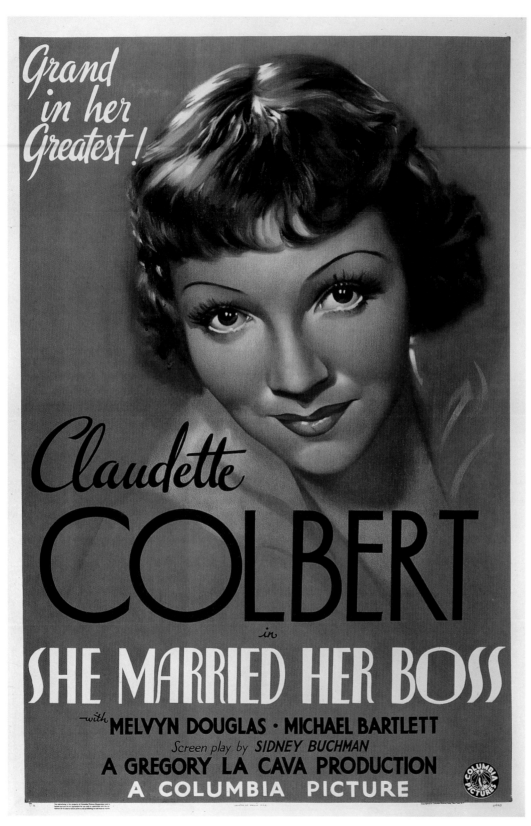

She Married Her Boss (1935)
US 41 × 27 in. (104 × 69 cm)
(Style A)

After Office Hours (1936)
US 41 × 27 in. (104 × 69 cm)
(Style C)

The Bitter Tea Of General Yen (1933)
US 41 × 27 in. (104 × 69 cm)

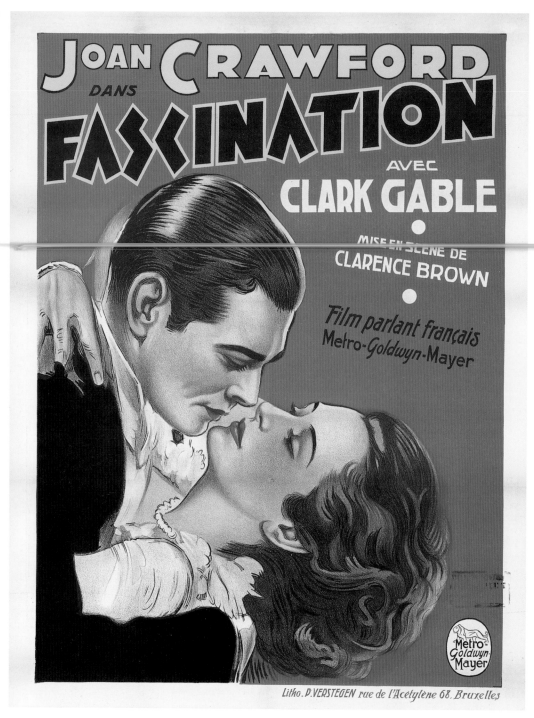

Chained (Fascination) (1934)
Belgian 31 × 24 in. (79 × 61 cm)

Bordertown (1935)
US 41 × 27 in. (104 × 69 cm)

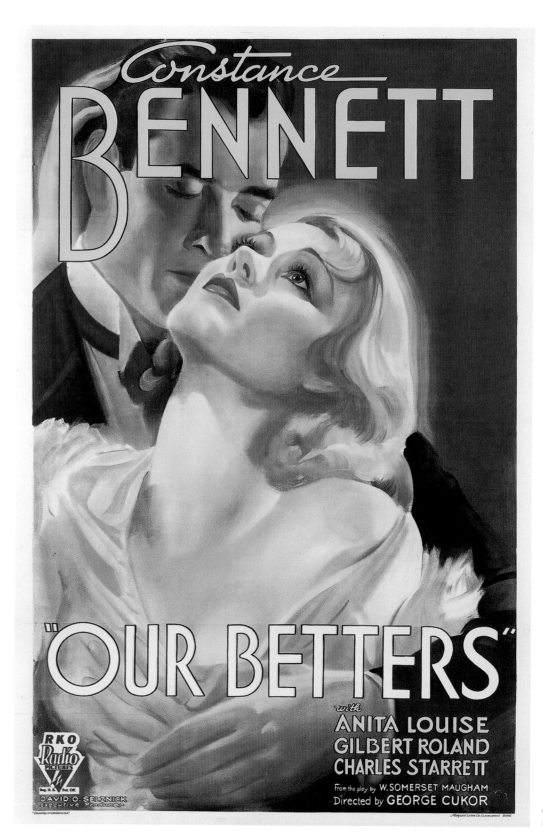

Our Betters (1933)
US 41 × 27 in. (104 × 69 cm)

JOSEPH M. SCHENCK presents
Constance
BENNETT
in
Moulin Rouge
with
FRANCHOT TONE
TULLIO CARMINATI
directed by SIDNEY LANFIELD
a DARRYL F. ZANUCK production
20TH CENTURY PICTURE
Released thru UNITED ARTISTS
LEASED TO THE EXHIBITOR BY UNITED ARTISTS CORPORATION

22

Flying Down To Rio (1933)
US 41 × 27 in. (104 × 69 cm)

Top Hat (1935)
US 41 × 27 in. (104 × 69 cm)
Art by Frederic C. Madan

42nd Street (1933)
US 41 × 27 in. (104 × 69 cm)
Art direction by Hubbard G. Robinson
& Joseph Tisman

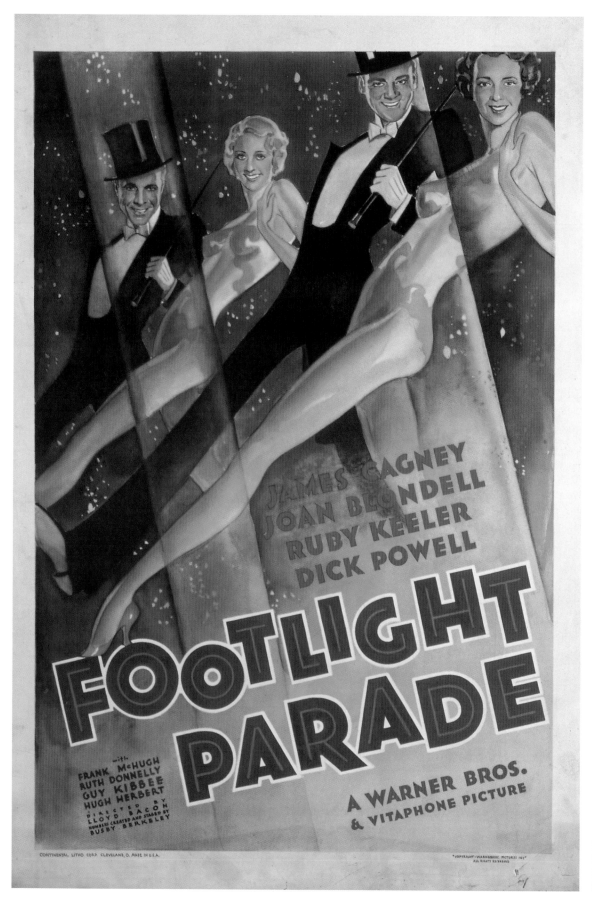

Footlight Parade (1933)
US 41 × 27 in. (104 × 69 cm)
Art direction by Hubbard G. Robinson
& Joseph Tisman

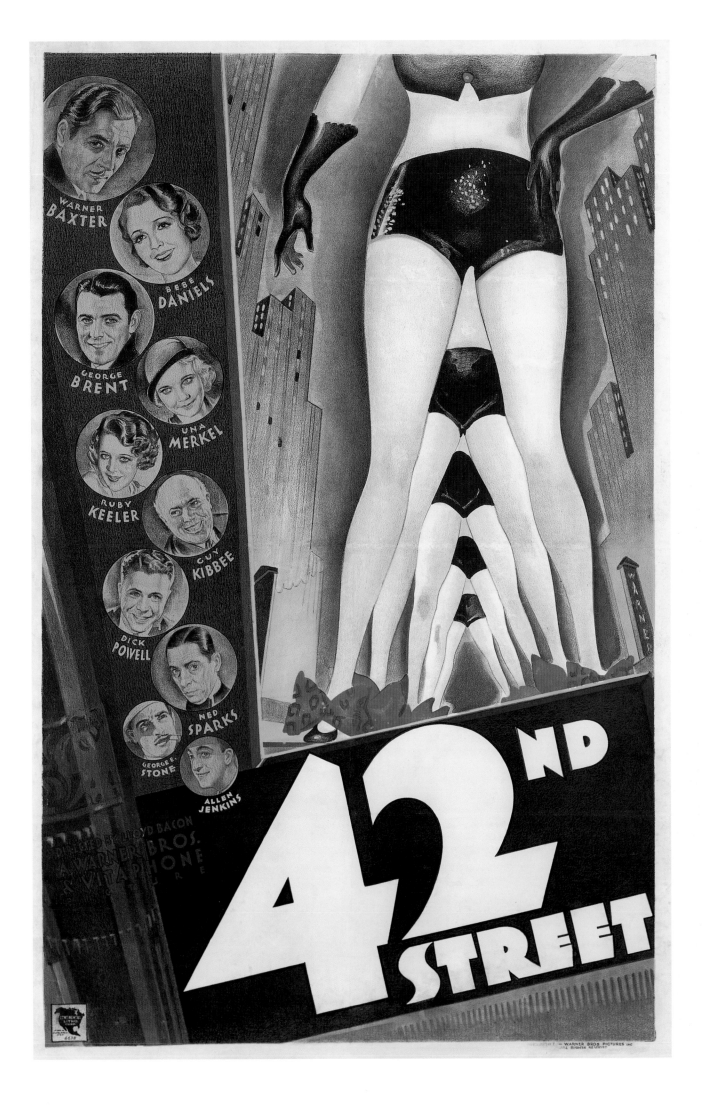

The Prisoner Of Swing (1938)
US 41 × 27 in. (104 × 69 cm)

The Wizard Of Oz (1939)
US 41 × 27 in. (104 × 69 cm)
(Style D)
Art by Al Hirschfeld

The Wizard Of Oz (1939)
US 14 × 9 in. (36 × 23 cm)

Gaiety! Glory! Glamour!

THE WIZARD OF OZ

with

JUDY GARLAND
FRANK MORGAN
RAY BOLGER
BERT LAHR
JACK HALEY

BILLIE BURKE
MARGARET HAMILTON
CHARLEY GRAPEWIN
and THE MUNCHKINS

A VICTOR FLEMING *Production*

SCREEN PLAY BY NOEL LANGLEY, FLORENCE RYERSON AND
EDGAR ALLAN WOOLF FROM THE BOOK BY L. FRANK BAUM

Directed by   *Produced by*
VICTOR FLEMING · MERVYN LEROY

It's
METRO-GOLDWYN-MAYER'S
TECHNICOLOR TRIUMPH!

LITHO IN U.S.A.   TOOKER LITHO CO. N.Y.

30

**The Wizard Of Oz
(Le Magicien D'Oz)** (1939)
French 63 × 94 in.
(160 × 239 cm)
Art by Boris Grinsson

King Kong (1933)
French 63 × 47 in. (160 × 119 cm)
(Style B)
Art by René Péron

King Kong (1933)
US 81 × 41 in. (206 × 104 cm)
(Style A)
Art by S. Barret McCormick & Bob Sisk
Art direction by David L. Strumf

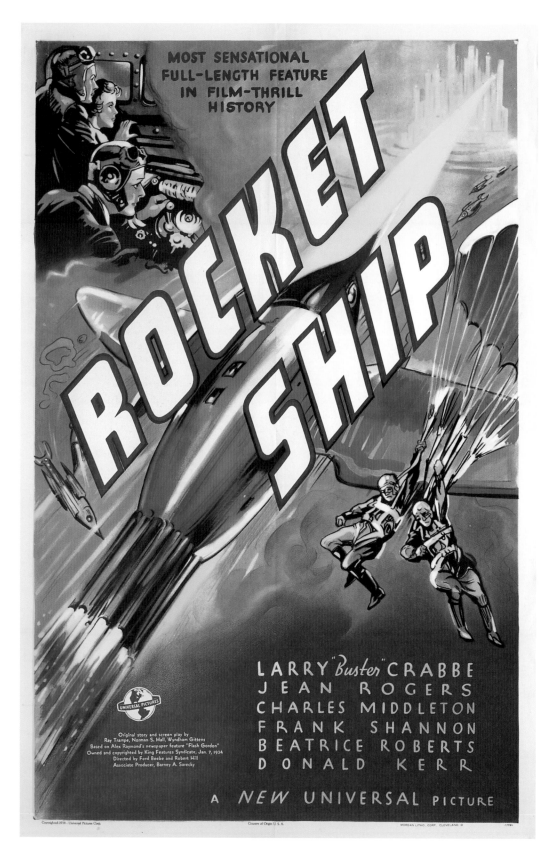

Rocket Ship (1938)
US 41 × 27 in. (104 × 69 cm)

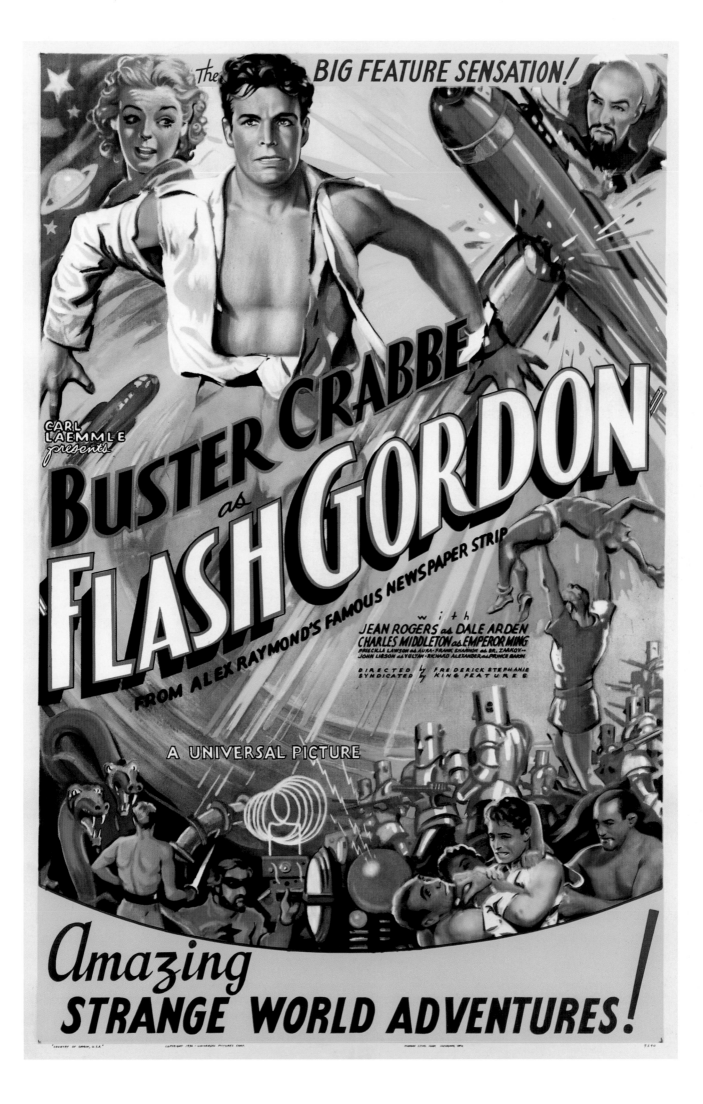

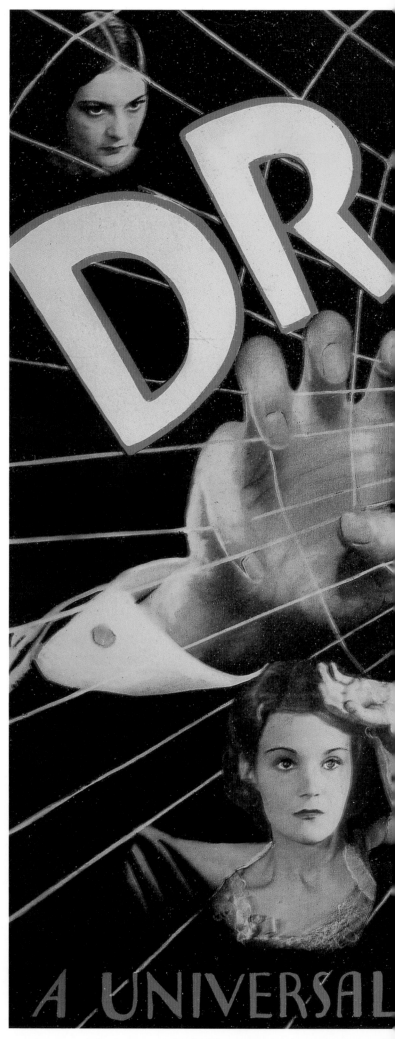

Dracula (1931)
US 22 × 28 in. (56 × 71 cm)

The Mummy (1932)
US 41 × 27 in. (104 × 69 cm)
(Style A)
Art by Karoly Grosz

Frankenstein (1931)
US 41 × 27 in. (104 × 69 cm)
Art by Karoly Grosz

**The Hunchback Of Notre Dame
(Quasimodo)** (1939)
French 63 × 94 in. (160 × 239 cm)
Art by Roland Coudon

uasimodo

le Chef d'Œuvre de Victor Hugo "Notre-Dame de Paris"

Mitchell - Maureen O'Hara - Edmond O'Brien

52, Av: des Champs-Elysées. PARIS

Gone With The Wind (1939)
US 41 × 27 in. (104 × 69 cm)
(Style CP)
Art by Armando Seguso

Gone With The Wind (1939)
US 41 × 27 in. (104 × 69 cm)
(Style DF)
Art by Armando Seguso
Art direction by Hal Burrows

DAVID O. SELZNICK'S *production of* MARGARET MITCHELL'S *Story of the Old South*

GONE WITH THE WIND

in TECHNICOLOR *Starring*

CLARK GABLE
as RHETT BUTLER

LESLIE **HOWARD** ☆ **DE HAVILLAND** OLIVIA

and presenting

VIVIEN LEIGH
as SCARLETT O'HARA

A SELZNICK INTERNATIONAL PICTURE
DIRECTED BY VICTOR FLEMING
SCREEN PLAY BY SIDNEY HOWARD
A METRO-GOLDWYN-MAYER *Release*
Music by Max Steiner

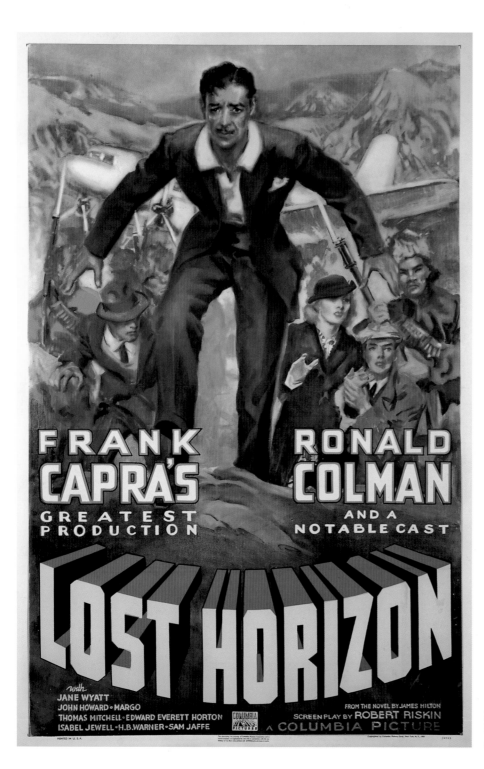

Lost Horizon (1937)
US 41 × 27 in. (104 × 69 cm)
Art by James Montgomery-Flagg

46

Cock Of The Air (1932)
US 41 × 27 in. (104 × 69 cm)
(Withdrawn)
Art attributed to Hap Hadley

Hell's Angels (1930)
US 81 × 41 in. (206 × 104 cm)
Art by Hap Hadley

HOWARD HUGHES

presents

COCK of the AIR

DIRECTED BY
TOM BUCKINGHAM

PRODUCED BY
HOWARD HUGHES

with
Chester Morris

M.R. LITHO. CO. N.Y.

LITHO. IN U.S.A.

Olympia 1. Teil – Fest Der Völker
(Den Stora Olympiaden / The Olympiad) (1939)
Swedish 39 × 27 in. (99 × 69 cm)
(Part I)

Olympia 2. Teil – Fest Der Völker
(Den Stora Olympiaden II: Dra Delen / The Olympiad) (1939)
Swedish 39 × 27 in. (99 × 69 cm)
(Part II)

Triumph des Willens

Reichsparteitagfilm der N·S·D·A·P·

Gesamtleitung u. Regie: Leni Riefenstahl

Offsetdruck August Scherl GmbH., Berlin SW 68 (Germany)

Secret Agent (1936)
US 41 × 27 in. (104 × 69 cm)

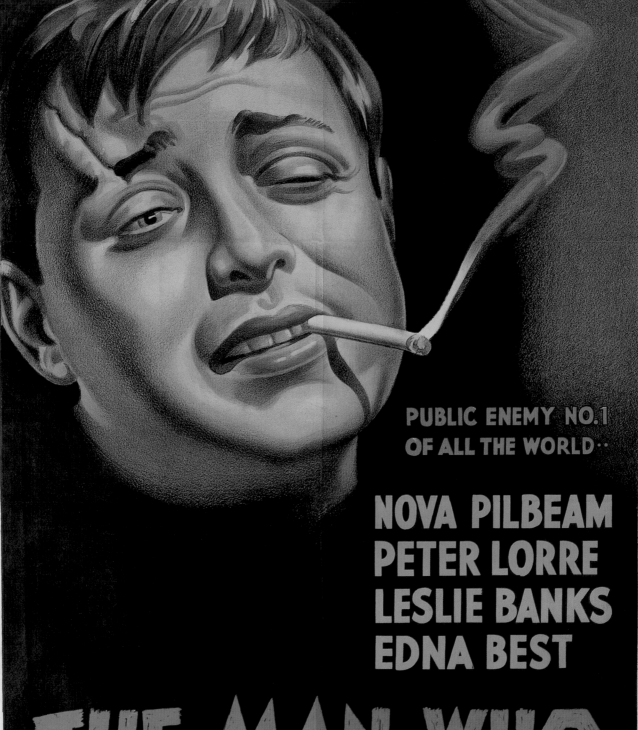

PUBLIC ENEMY NO.1
OF ALL THE WORLD··

NOVA PILBEAM
PETER LORRE
LESLIE BANKS
EDNA BEST

THE MAN WHO
KNEW TOO MUCH

A  PRODUCTION

Directed by ALFRED HITCHCOCK

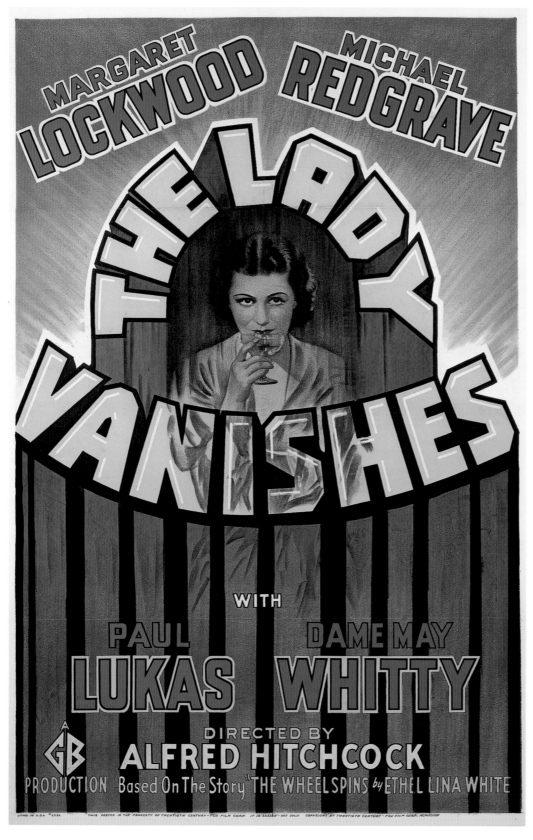

The Lady Vanishes (1938)
US 41 × 27 in. (104 × 69 cm)

The 39 Steps (1935)
British 87 × 40 in. (221 × 102 cm)
(Style A)
Art by Mark Stone

The Thin Man (1934)
US 41 × 27 in. (104 × 69 cm)
(Style D)
Art by Ted Ireland 'Vincentini'

The Benson Murder Case (1930)
US 36 × 14 in. (91 × 36 cm)

The Kennel Murder Case (1933)
US 41 × 27 in. (104 × 69 cm)
Art direction by Anthony Gablik
& Joseph Tisman

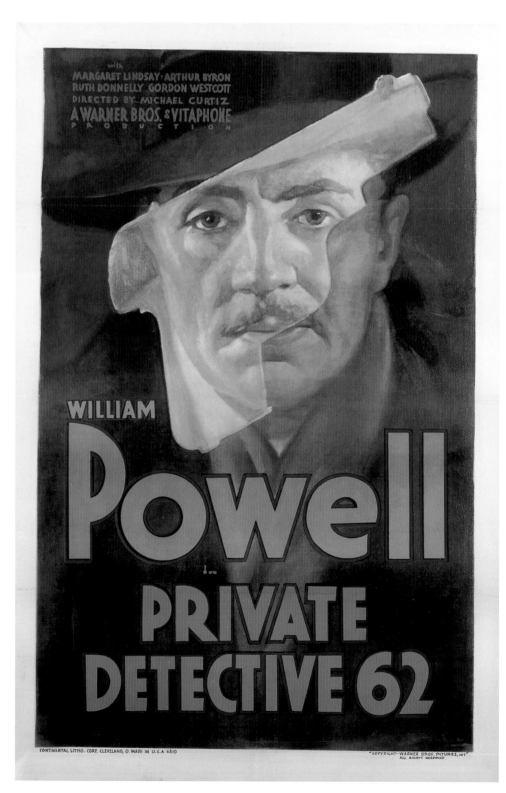

Private Detective 62 (1933)
US 41 × 27 in. (104 × 69 cm)
Art direction by Anthony Gablik
& Joseph Tisman

WILLIAM

POWELL

RETURNS AS
**PHILO
VANCE**

in

S.S. VAN DINE'S

**THE KENNEL
MURDER
CASE**

with
MARY ASTOR · EUGENE PALLETTE
HELEN VINSON · RALPH MORGAN
JACK LaRUE · PAUL CAVANAUGH
DIRECTED BY
MICHAEL CURTIZ
A WARNER BROS.
& VITAPHONE PICTURE

CONTINENTAL LITHO. CORP. CLEVELAND, O. MADE IN U.S.A. 6482

"COPYRIGHT WARNER BROS. PICTURES INC."
ALL RIGHTS RESERVED

The Hound Of The Baskervilles (1939)
US 41 × 27 in. (104 × 69 cm)
Art direction by S. Barret & McCormick

**The Adventures Of Sherlock Holmes
(Sherlock Holmes)** (1939)
French 47 × 31 in. (119 × 79 cm)
Art by Jacques Bonneaud

**Le Testament Du Dr. Mabuse
(The Last Will Of Dr. Mabuse)** (1933)
French 31 × 24 in. (79 × 61 cm)

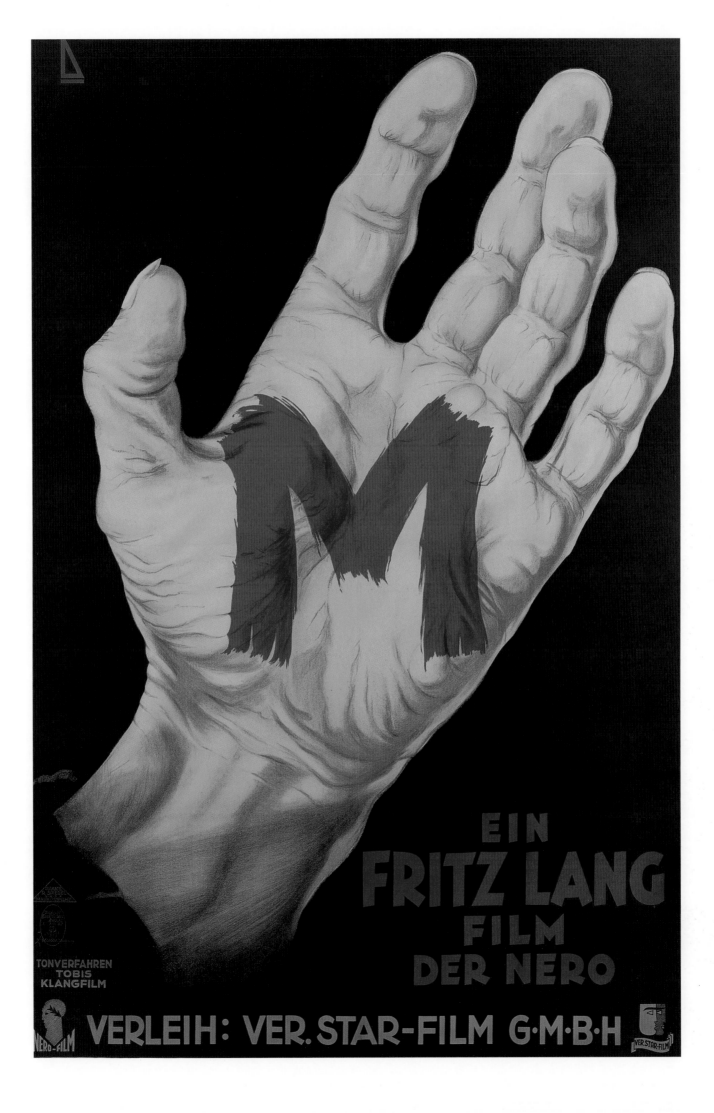

62

The Public Enemy (1931)
US 22 × 14 in. (56 × 36 cm)
Art direction by Anthony Gablik
& Joseph Tisman

'G' Men (1935)
US 81 × 41 in. (206 × 104 cm)
Art direction by Anthony Gablik
& Joseph Tisman

HUMPHREY BOGART
SYLVIA SIDNEY
JOEL McCREA

en

PUNTO
MUERTO

Una producción de
SAMUEL GOLDWYN
distribuido por
GUARANTEED
PICTURES
LAVALLE 1943   47.2.33
BUENOS AIRES

Dead End (Punto Muerto) (1937)
Argentine 42 × 56 in. (107 × 142 cm)
Art by Osvaldo Venturi

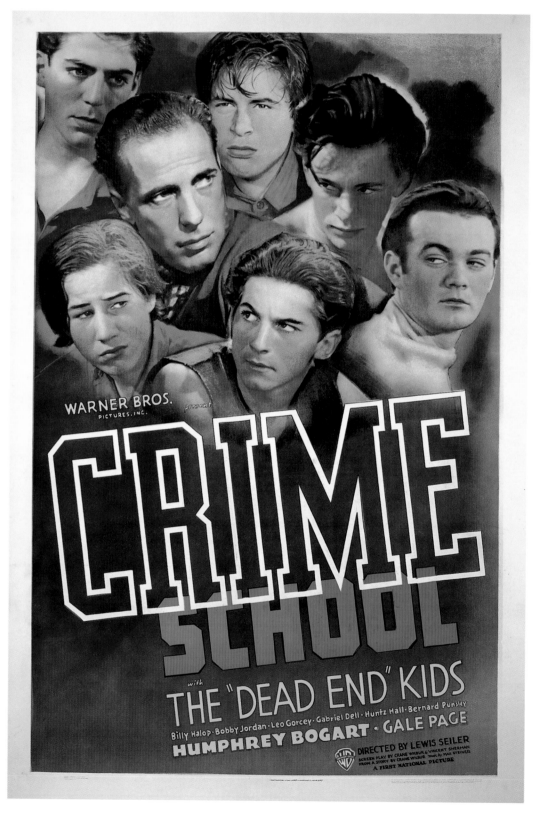

Crime School (1938)
US 41 × 27 in. (104 × 69 cm)

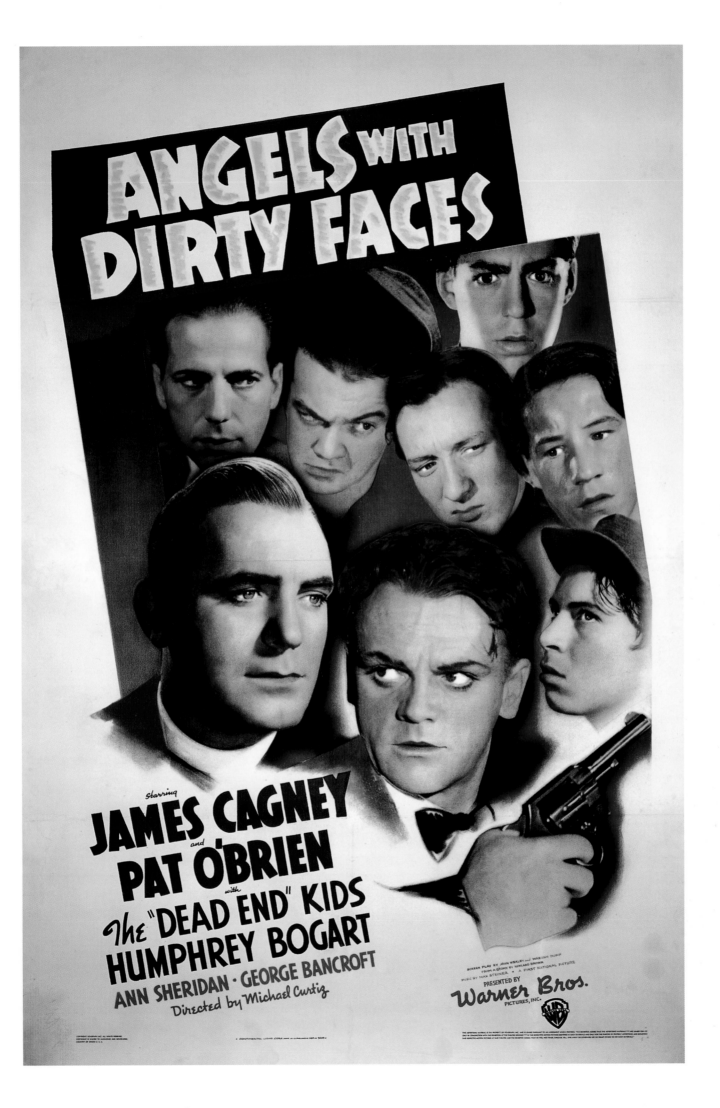

Scarface (1932)
US 22 × 28 in. (56 × 71 cm)

with

PAUL MUNI
OSGOOD PERKINS
KAREN MORLEY
ANN DVORAK

Adapted by **BEN HECHT**
from the novel by Armitage Trail
A
HOWARD HAWKS
PRODUCTION
UNITED ARTISTS PICTURE

R·FACE

Swing (1938)
US 41 × 27 in. (104 × 69 cm)

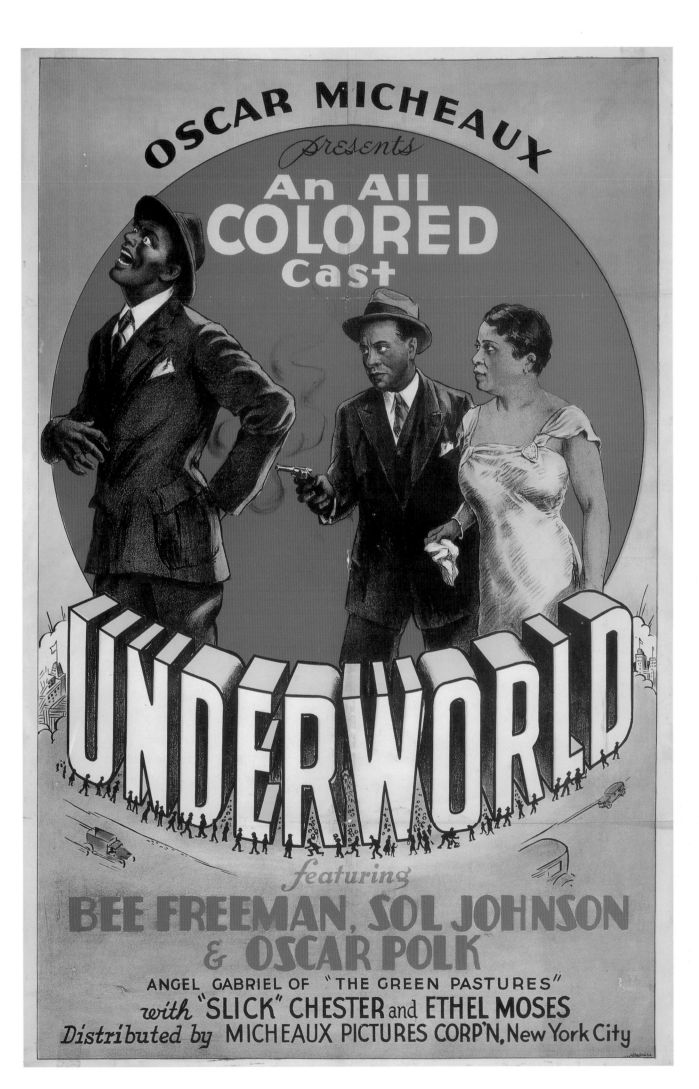

Sanders Of The River
(Bosambo) (1935)
Argentine 42 × 28 in. (107 × 71 cm)
Art by Osvaldo Venturi

Emperor Jones (1933)
US 41 × 27 in. (104 × 69 cm)

JOHN KRIMSKY and
GIFFORD COCHRAN
present

PAUL ROBESON

IN

Emperor

JONES

WITH
DUDLEY DIGGES

FROM THE STAGE PLAY BY
EUGENE O'NEILL
Directed by DUDLEY MURPHY

Released Thru
UNITED ARTISTS

The Oregon Trail (1936)
US 41 × 27 in. (104 × 69 cm)

Cimarron (1930)
US 41 × 27 in. (104 × 69 cm)
Art by Frederick C. Madan
Art direction by David L. Strump

A Powerful Story
of 9 Strange People

STAGECOACH

A
WALTER WANGER
PRODUCTION
Directed by
JOHN FORD

with

CLAIRE TREVOR · JOHN WAYNE · ANDY DEVINE
JOHN CARRADINE · THOMAS MITCHELL · LOUISE PLATT · GEORGE BANCROFT
DONALD MEEK · BERTON CHURCHILL · TIM HOLT

Released Thru
UNITED ARTISTS

78

Ridin' For Justice (1932)
US 41 × 27 in. (104 × 69 cm)

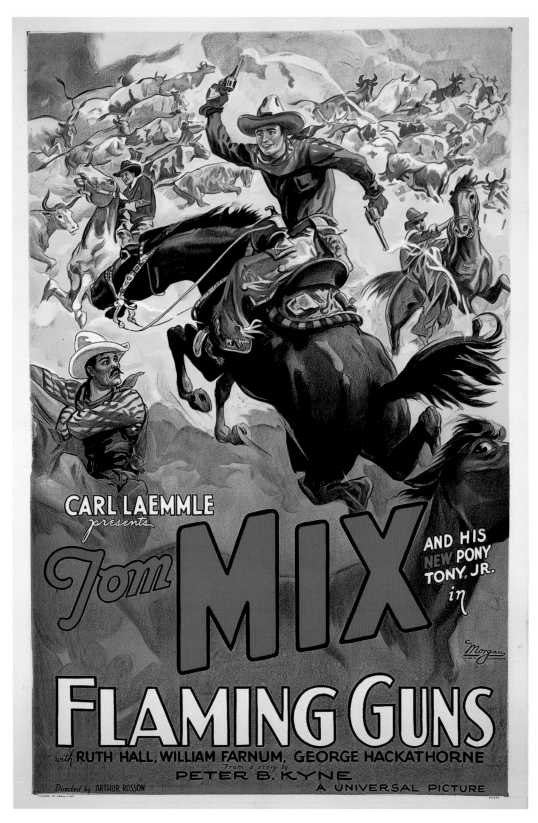

Beau Geste (1939)
US 41 × 27 in. (104 × 69 cm)
(Style B)
Art direction by Vincent Trotta
& Maurice Kallis

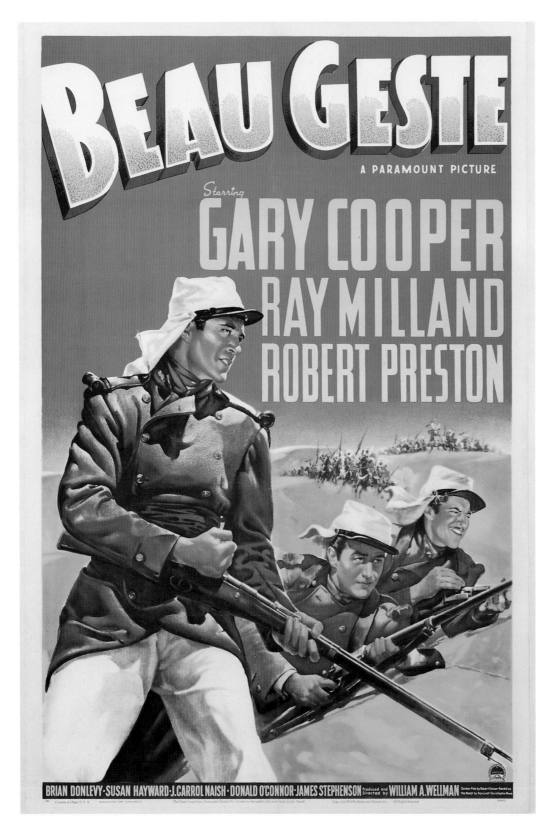

Beau Geste (1939)
US 41 × 27 in. (104 × 69 cm)
(Style A)
Art direction by Vincent Trotta
& Maurice Kallis

82

The Adventures Of Robin Hood (1938)
US 41 × 27 in. (104 × 69 cm)

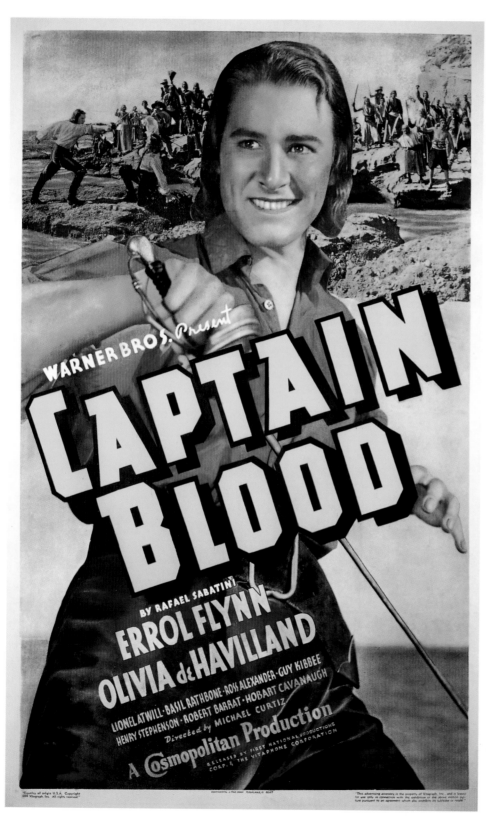

Captain Blood (1935)
US 41 × 27 in. (104 × 69 cm)
Art direction by Anthony Gablik
& Joseph Tisman

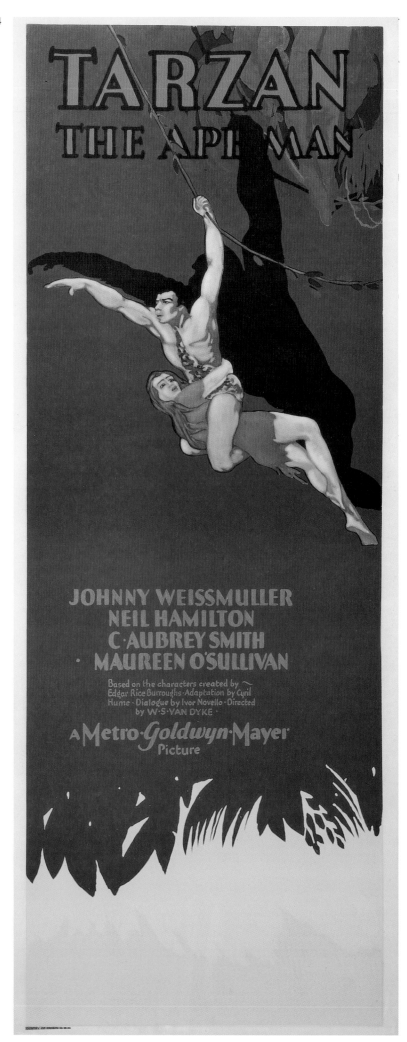

Tarzan And His Mate (1934)
US 41 × 27 in. (104 × 69 cm)
(Style C)
Art by William Galbraith Crawford

Tarzan The Ape Man (1932)
US 36 × 14 in. (91 × 36 cm)

Extase (1932)
French 63 × 94 in. (160 × 239 cm)
Art by Roger Vacher

A Woman Commands (1932)
US 81 × 41 in. (206 × 104 cm)

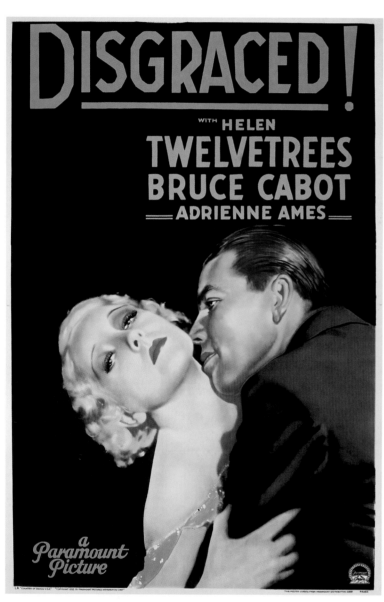

Disgraced! (1933)
US 41 × 27 in. (104 × 69 cm)
(Style A)

Virtue (1932)
US 41 × 27 in. (104 × 69 cm)
(Style A)

The Sin Of Nora Moran (1933)
US 41 × 27 in. (104 × 69 cm)
Art by Albert Vargas

Majestic Pictures presents

The SIN of NORA MORAN

with

ZITA JOHANN • JOHN MILJAN • ALAN DINEHART
CLAIRE DuBREY • PAUL CAVANAGH

PRESENTED IN
A NEW MARVELOUS SCREEN TECHNIQUE
Directed by **PHIL GOLDSTONE**

Slaves In Bondage (1937)
US 41 × 27 in. (104 × 69 cm)

Duck Soup (1933)
US 22 × 28 in. (56 × 71 cm)
(Style A)

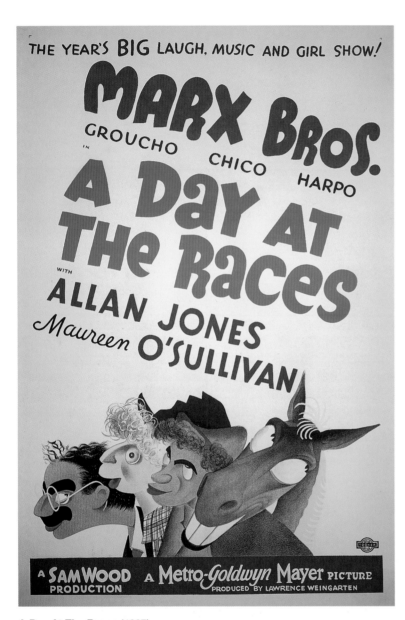

A Day At The Races (1937)
US 41 × 27 in. (104 × 69 cm)
(Style C)
Art by Al Hirschfeld

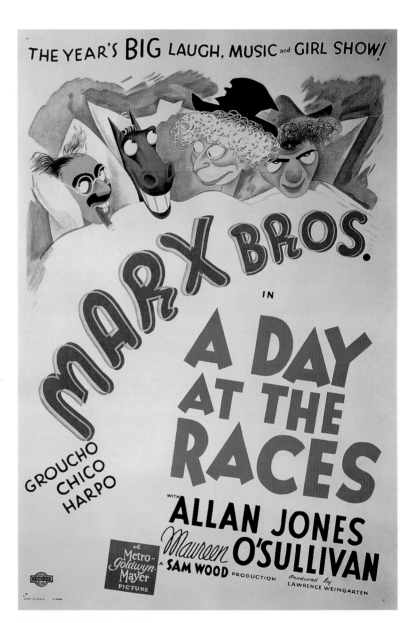

A Day At The Races (1937)
US 41 × 27 in. (104 × 69 cm)
(Style D)
Art by Al Hirschfeld

A Night At The Opera (1935)
US 41 × 27 in. (104 × 69 cm)
(Style C)
Art by Al Hirschfeld

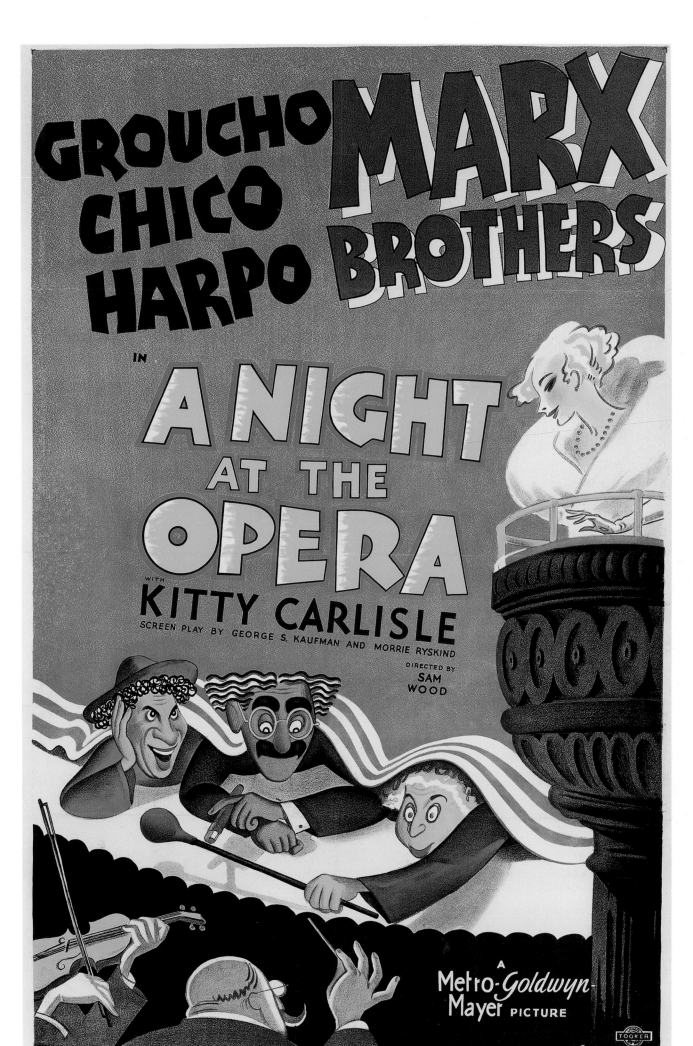

The Big Idea (1934)
US 41 × 27 in. (104 × 69 cm)
Art by Al Hirschfeld

Hello Pop (1933)
US 41 × 27 in. (104 × 69 cm)
Art by Al Hirschfeld

Beau Hunks (1931)
US 41 × 27 in. (104 × 69 cm)
Art by Al Hirschfeld

Pack Up Your Troubles (1932)
US 41 × 27 in. (104 × 69 cm)
Art by Al Hirschfeld

Another Fine Mess (1930)
US 41 × 27 in. (104 × 69 cm)
Art by Al Hirschfeld

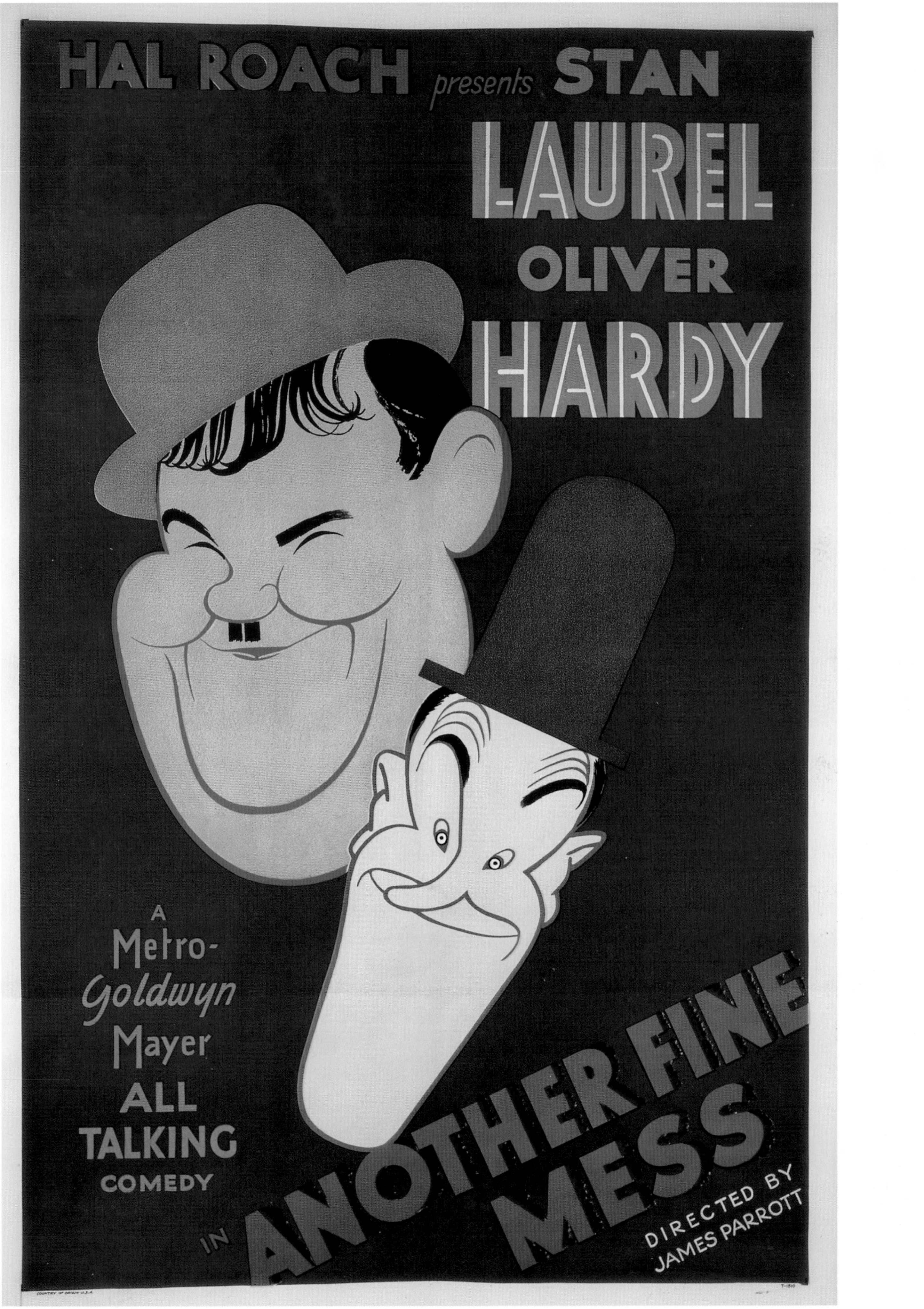
HAL ROACH presents STAN
LAUREL
OLIVER
HARDY
A
Metro-
Goldwyn
Mayer
ALL
TALKING
COMEDY
IN
ANOTHER FINE
MESS
DIRECTED BY
JAMES PARROTT

City Lights (1931)
US 81 × 41 in. (206 × 104 cm)

City Lights (1931)
US 41 × 27 in. (104 × 69 cm)
(Style B)
Art by Hap Hadley

A Nous La Liberté (1931)
French 63 × 94 in. (160 × 239 cm)
Art by Jean Adrien Mercier

Quatorze Juillet (14 Juillet) (1933)
French 63 × 46 in. (160 × 117 cm)
Art by Jean Adrien Mercier

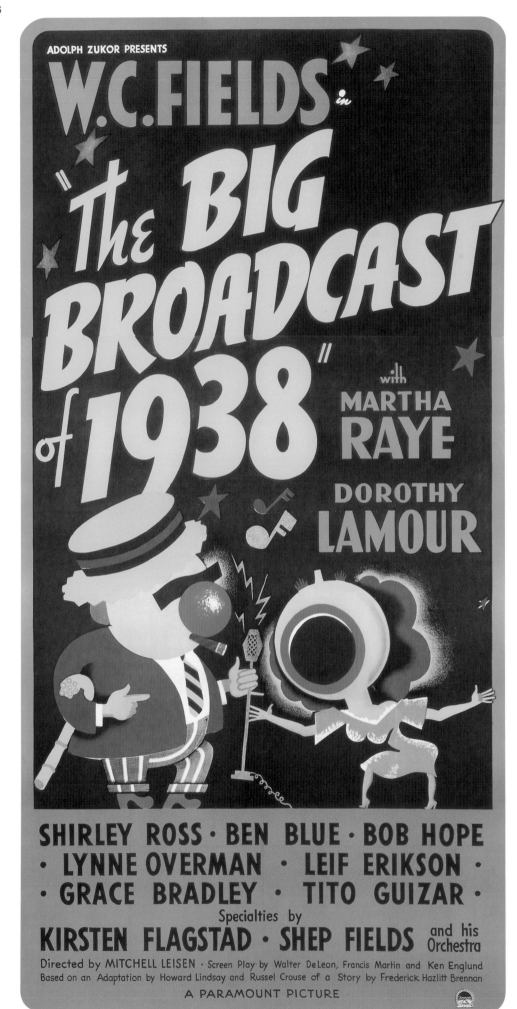

The Big Broadcast Of 1938 (1938)
US 81 × 41 in. (206 × 104 cm)
(Style A)
Art by Jacques Kapralik
Art direction by Vincent Trotta
& Maurice Kallis

MAURICE
CHEVALIER
IN
'THE WAY TO LOVE'
WITH
ANN DVORAK
EDWARD EVERETT HORTON
Directed by NORMAN TAUROG

a Paramount Picture

It's A Gift (1934)
US 41 × 27 in. (104 × 69 cm)
(Style A)
Art direction by Vincent Trotta
& Maurice Kallis

Baby, Takes A Bow (1934)
US 41 × 27 in. (104 × 69 cm)

Clive Of India (1935)
US 41 × 27 in. (104 × 69 cm)
(Leader Press)

Riffraff (1936)
US 41 × 27 in. (104 × 69 cm)
(Leader Press)

Blonde Venus (1932)
US 36 × 14 in. (91 × 36 cm)

Morocco (1930)
US 41 × 27 in. (104 × 69 cm)
(Style B)

The Devil Is A Woman (1935)
US 41 × 27 in. (104 × 69 cm)
(Style A)

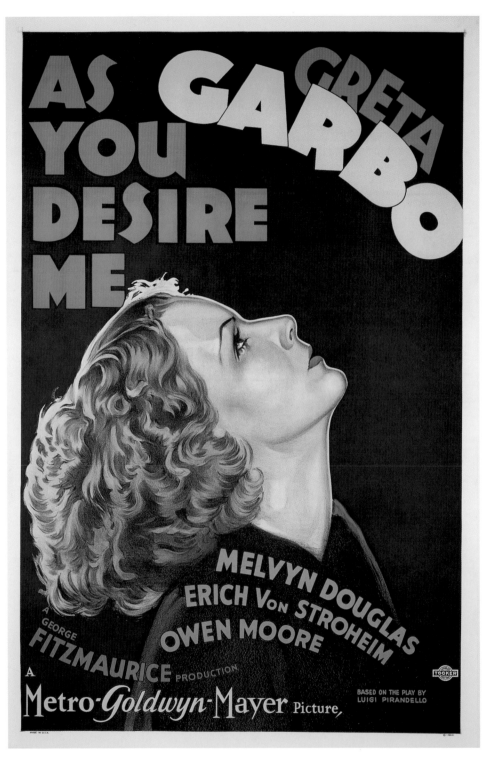

As You Desire Me (1932)
US 41 × 27 in. (104 × 69 cm)

Mata Hari (1931)
Czech 33 × 23 in. (84 × 58 cm)

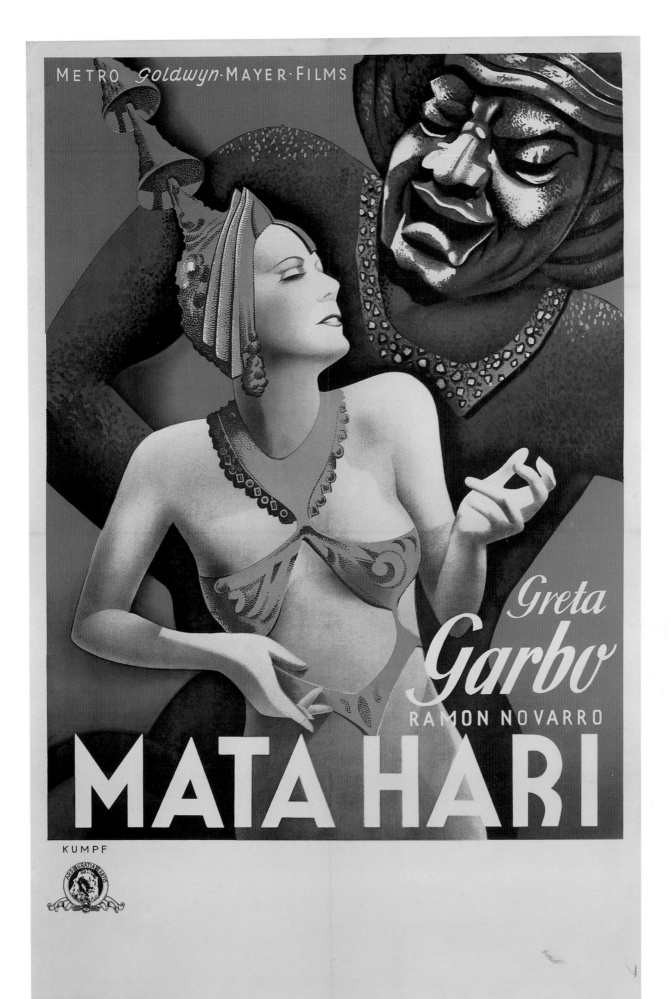

Red-Headed Woman (1932)
US 41 × 27 in. (104 × 69 cm)

The Woman In Red (1935)
US 41 × 27 in. (104 × 69 cm)

Jezebel (1938)
US 41 × 27 in. (104 × 69 cm)
Art direction by Anthony Gablik
& Joseph Tisman

Bette
DAVIS
JEZEBEL

with

HENRY FONDA   GEORGE BRENT

MARGARET LINDSAY   DONALD CRISP   FAY BAINTER

RICHARD CROMWELL   HENRY O'NEIL   SPRING BYINGTON   JOHN LITEL

A **WILLIAM WYLER** PRODUCTION

SCREEN PLAY BY CLEMENTS RIPLEY, ABEM FINKEL & JOHN HUSTON FROM THE PLAY BY OWEN DAVIS, SR.   MUSIC BY MAX STEINER

A WARNER BROS. PICTURE

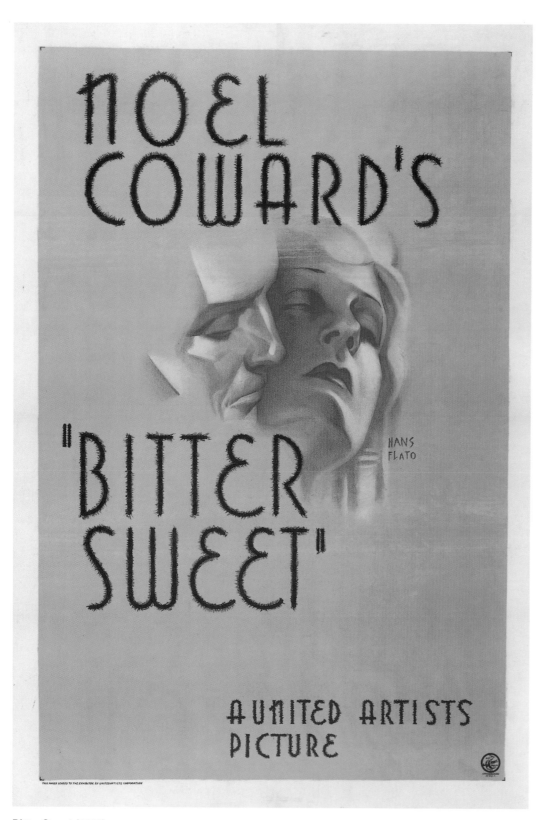

Bitter Sweet (1933)
US 41 × 27 in. (104 × 69 cm)
Art by Hans Flato

Dodsworth (Infedeltà) (1936)
Italian 79 × 55 in. (201 × 140 cm)
Art by Anselmo Ballester

BALLESTER
RUTH CHATTERTON
WALTER HUSTON
MARY ASTOR
PAUL LUKAS
Infedeltà
TRATTO DAL FAMOSO ROMANZO "DODSWORTH"
DI SINCLAR LEWIS DIRETTO DA WILLIAM WYLER
UNITED ARTISTS
ARTISTI ASSOCIATI
PRODUZIONE
SAMUEL GOLDWYN
A.P.E. ROMA

Little Caesar (1931)
Belgian 31 × 24 in. (79 × 61 cm)

PARAMOUNT présente

GARY
COOPER
SYLVIA
SYDNEY
DANS

LES CARREFOURS
DE LA VILLE
C'est un film Paramount

CINÉ-STUDIO tél. 26.45.04 Bruxelles

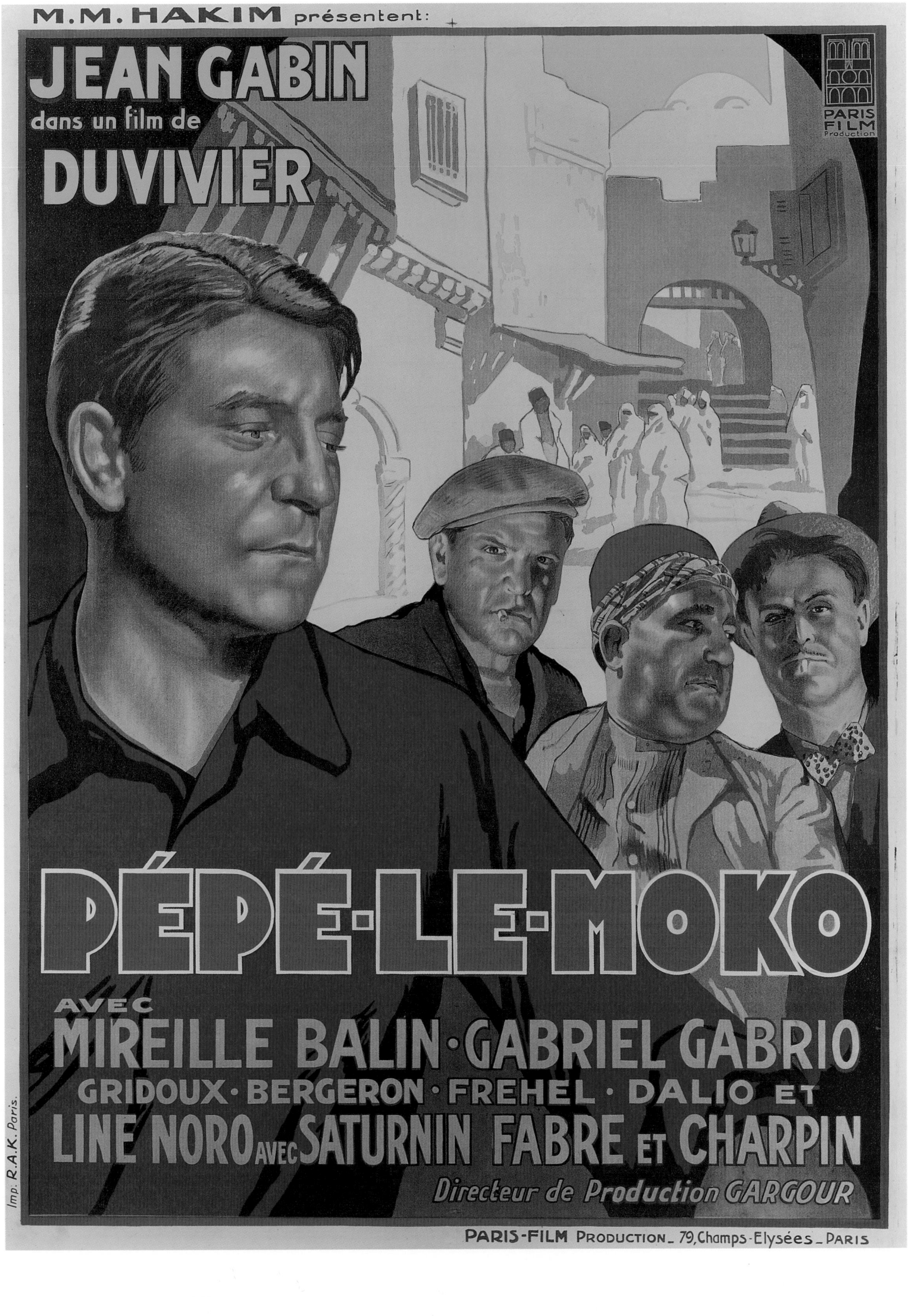
M.M. HAKIM présentent:
JEAN GABIN
dans un film de
DUVIVIER
PARIS FILM Production
PÉPÉ-LE-MOKO
AVEC
MIREILLE BALIN · GABRIEL GABRIO
GRIDOUX · BERGERON · FREHEL · DALIO ET
LINE NORO AVEC SATURNIN FABRE ET CHARPIN
Directeur de Production GARGOUR
Imp. R.A.K. Paris.
PARIS-FILM PRODUCTION _ 79, Champs-Elysées _ PARIS